ACTION SPORTS

ZIP LINES

Kelli Hicks

ROURKE PUBLISHING

Vero Beach, Florida 32964

www.rourkepublishing.com

PHOTO CREDITS: © Durden Images: cover; © Annetje: title page; © Cornelis Opstal: pages 2-3; © frantisekhojdysz: page 5; © Wolfgang Amri: page 6; © Sergiy Zavgorodny: page 7; © Associated Press: page 8; © Jason Maehl: page 10; © Fukuoka Irina: page 11; © Wolfgang Steiner: page 12; © Elisei Shafer: page 13; © oksana.perkins: page 15; © Dropu: pages 16-17; © RCB Shooter: pages 18-19; © Rich Carey: pages 21, 22

Edited by Jeanne Sturm

Cover designed by Tara Raymo
Interior designed by Renee Brady

Library of Congress Cataloging-in-Publication Data

Hicks, Kelli Shay.
 Zip lines / Kelli Hicks.
     p. cm. -- (Action sports)
 Includes index.
 ISBN 978-1-60694-359-5
 1. Zip lines--Juvenile literature. I. Title.
 GV200.57.H53 2009
 796.46--dc22
                                        2009013577

Printed in the USA
CG/CG

ROURKE PUBLISHING

www.rourkepublishing.com - rourke@rourkepublishing.com
Post Office Box 643328 Vero Beach, Florida 32964

TABLE OF CONTENTS

EXTREME SPORTS

Many people are familiar with extreme sports. Skateboarding, snow boarding, and BMX have all become popular with adventure seekers. Now, many of those who enjoy outdoor adventures are looking to zip lines to satisfy their need for danger and excitement.

Extreme sports participants enjoy taking risks and having fun!

WHAT IS A ZIP LINE?

Also called flying foxes, zip lines are often found on children's play equipment or on a playground. A zip line is a **pulley suspended** on some type of heavy **inclined** wire or cable. The rider holds on to the pulley, and **gravity** pulls the rider down the length of the zip line.

An old tire with a seat is a creative way to help a passenger travel the length of a zip line on a playground.

Some zip line rides end with a splash! Parks or campgrounds that have a lake with a swimming area might have a zip line that zips you from dry land and into the lake.

SAFETУ CHECK

Every zip line tour begins with a safety check. Participants must wear hiking shoes, boots, or some type of athletic shoe that covers their feet, as well as helmets to protect their heads. Adventurers are fitted with a **harness** based on their size and weight. The chest harness hooks in front of the body and has straps that fit around the legs to provide a makeshift seat. Many times, guides give participants jackets to wear. Instructors tighten the harness to be sure that it will support the rider's body.

A tight-fitting harness is necessary to support the weight of a zip line passenger. Guides will always check to ensure a proper fit.

Many people feel scared or nervous the first time they speed down the cable of a zip line.

Each adventurer also receives a **trolley**. The trolley is a metal bar that attaches to the zip line and is essential for moving a rider down the line. The trolley type is also based on the size and weight of the person.

This metal trolley attaches to the cable and has handlebars to make it easy for the passenger to maintain his grip.

Did You Know?

Since many zip lines are attached to the tops of trees or up in the mountains, a hike to get to the launch **platform** or tower may be necessary. Even though the temperature at the bottom of the climb is warm, it can get cooler the higher you go.

KAPALUA ADVENTURE TOURS

On a trip to Hawaii, you can visit the island of Maui and take an adventure in the town of Kapalua. First, ride in a **unimog** past scenic pineapple fields to 1,400 feet (427 meters) above sea level. As you look out you will have an amazing view of the island of Maui. Climb to the top of a man-made tower. Feel the wind as it whips past your face, and feel your heart begin to race.

As you step off the edge of the tower, you can look at the nature all around as you race down the 985 feet (300 meters) of wire. One zip line on this tour even zips you 2,300 feet (701 meters) from beginning to end over a valley filled with native plants. You might even spot a waterfall.

Guides receive hours of extensive training to be able to demonstrate proper form and handle any emergency that might arise.

HOW DO YOU STOP?

You might be wondering how you stop at the end of the zip line without getting hurt. Depending on the level of the incline and the size of the landing **platform**, there are several types of **braking** systems. For low speeds and a slight incline, you might use a hand brake. You would wear a thick glove and squeeze the cable to come to a stop.

Guides wait at the end of each zip in order to assist passengers onto and off of the platform.

Children who want to travel on a zip line must be heavy enough for gravity to carry them the length of the cable.

Did You Know?

Many families experience zip line tours while vacationing. Even children can zip over the canopy of the rain forest, canyons, and valleys of the Hawaiian Islands, or the rain forests of South America.

On longer, faster, or steeper lines, where riders are **suspended** too low to be able to grab the line, a **mechanical** braking system helps bring the rider to a stop.

As the riders approach the end of the line, they hit a block made of wood and polyurethane that acts as a shock absorber. The block hits a spring at the end of the line that stops the motion of the riders. The newest type of braking system is magnetic. It provides a smooth stop for riders traveling at even the fastest speeds.

Special trolleys can be used to support the weight of two people riding together, or riding tandem.

RAIN FOREST TOURS

Visitors in South America might use a zip line to get a unique perspective of the rain forest. Adventurers hike through the forest to reach platforms built at various heights. Participants zip from one platform to another and are able to see and hear many different species of rain forest animals.

Zip lines offer a unique perspective of the rain forest.

Taking pictures while suspended in mid-air is a great way to capture the beauty of nature all around.

PROTECTING THE ENVIRONMENT

Companies that offer zip line tours make every effort to preserve the natural beauty of the environment with the least amount of disturbance to the plants and animals in those areas. Guides lead visitors through the least populated areas and may tie back plants rather than cut them out of the way. Travelers use limited pathways to produce the least amount of erosion or destruction to the grounds.

Bridges made from natural materials help travelers get from one zip line to the next without harm to the native plants.

Rain forest zip tours can help teach people about the importance of the rain forest environment.

ARE YOU UP TO THE CHALLENGE?

Whether you are zipping over the rain forest, above valleys and canyons, through the mountains, or as part of a challenge course, a zip line is an action adventure that allows you to see the beauty of the outdoors while flying through the air. Are you up to the challenge?

Glossary

braking (brayk-ing): stopping or slowing down using a device

gravity (GRAV-uh-tee): the force that pulls things down toward the Earth and keeps them from floating away into space

harness (HAR-niss): a set of straps or pieces used to keep someone safe

inclined (in-KLINDE): leaning, or sloping

mechanical (mun-KAN-uh-kuhl): operated by machinery

platform (PLAT-form): a flat, raised structure where people can stand

pulley (PUL-ee): a lifting machine made from a rope, chain, or cable

suspended (suh-SPEND-ed): something attached to a support so that it hangs downward

trolley (TROL-ee): a metal device that hooks the rider to the cable on a zip line

unimog (YOO-nuh-mog): an off road vehicle designed for jungle, mountain, and desert terrain

Index

Websites

adventuretravel.about.com/od/ecotourism/ht/howtozipline.htm

adventuretravel.about.com/od/treetopaboveadventures/a/canopytours.htm

www.mos.org/sln/Leonardo/InventorsToolbox.html

About the Author

Kelli Hicks is a teacher who has learned to enjoy action adventures like sliding down a zip line at top speed (thanks to the awesome guides in Maui)! She lives in Tampa with her husband and daughter and hopes to glide down a zip line again soon!